Views of Africa

Discover the continent that is as diverse
as it is magnificent

ENCYCLOPÆDIA

Britannica®

CHICAGO   LONDON   NEW DELHI   PARIS   SEOUL   SYDNEY   TAIPEI   TOKYO

© 2004 BY ENCYCLOPÆDIA BRITANNICA, INC.

Cover photos (front): Anthony Bannister—Gallo Images/Corbis; (back): Sharna Balfour—Gallo Images/Corbis. Cover insert photos (left): Roger Wood/Corbis; (centre): Lawson Wood/Corbis; (right): Robert Holmes/Corbis.

International Standard Book Number: 1-59339-042-4

No part of this work may be reproduced or utilized in any form or by any means, electronic or mechanical, including photocopying, recording, or by any information storage and retrieval system, without permission in writing from the publisher.

BRITANNICA LEARNING LIBRARY: VIEWS OF AFRICA 2004

Britannica.com may be accessed on the Internet at http://www.britannica.com.

(Trademark Reg. U.S. Pat. Off.) Printed in Singapore.

Views of Africa

I N T R O D U C T I O N

Who were the pharaohs? What country was created as a home for freed slaves? On what river would you find the Aswan High Dam? What was apartheid?

In ***Views of Africa,*** you'll discover answers to these questions and many more. Through pictures, articles, and fun facts, you'll learn about the people, traditions, landscapes, and history that make up many of the countries and cities of Africa.

To help you on your journey, we've provided the following signposts in *Views of Africa*:

■ **Subject Tabs**—The coloured box in the upper corner of each right-hand page will quickly tell you the article subject.

■ **Search Lights**—Try these mini-quizzes before and after you read the article and see how much - *and how quickly* - you can learn. You can even make this a game with a reading partner. (Answers are upside down at the bottom of one of the pages.)

■ **Did You Know?**—Check out these fun facts about the article subject. With these surprising 'factoids', you can entertain your friends, impress your teachers, and amaze your parents.

■ **Picture Captions**—Read the captions that go with the photos. They provide useful information about the article subject.

■ **Vocabulary**—New or difficult words are in **bold type**. You'll find them explained in the Glossary at the end of the book.

■ **Learn More!**—Follow these pointers to related articles in the book. These articles are listed in the Table of Contents and appear on the Subject Tabs.

■ **Maps**—You'll find lots of information in this book's many maps.

　■ The **Country Maps** point out national capitals. **Globes** beside Subject Tabs show where countries are located in the world.

　■ The **Continent Maps** have a number key showing the location of all countries.

■ The **Icons** on the maps highlight major geographic features and climate. Here's a key to what the map icons mean:

☀	Deserts and Other Dry Areas	🌴	Rainforests
❄	Polar Regions and Other Frozen Areas	🌳	General Forests
⛰	Mountains		

The rocky islands of Seychelles are rugged and beautiful.
© Nik Wheeler/Corbis

Views of Africa

TABLE OF CONTENTS

Britannica®

LEARNING LIBRARY

Have a great trip!

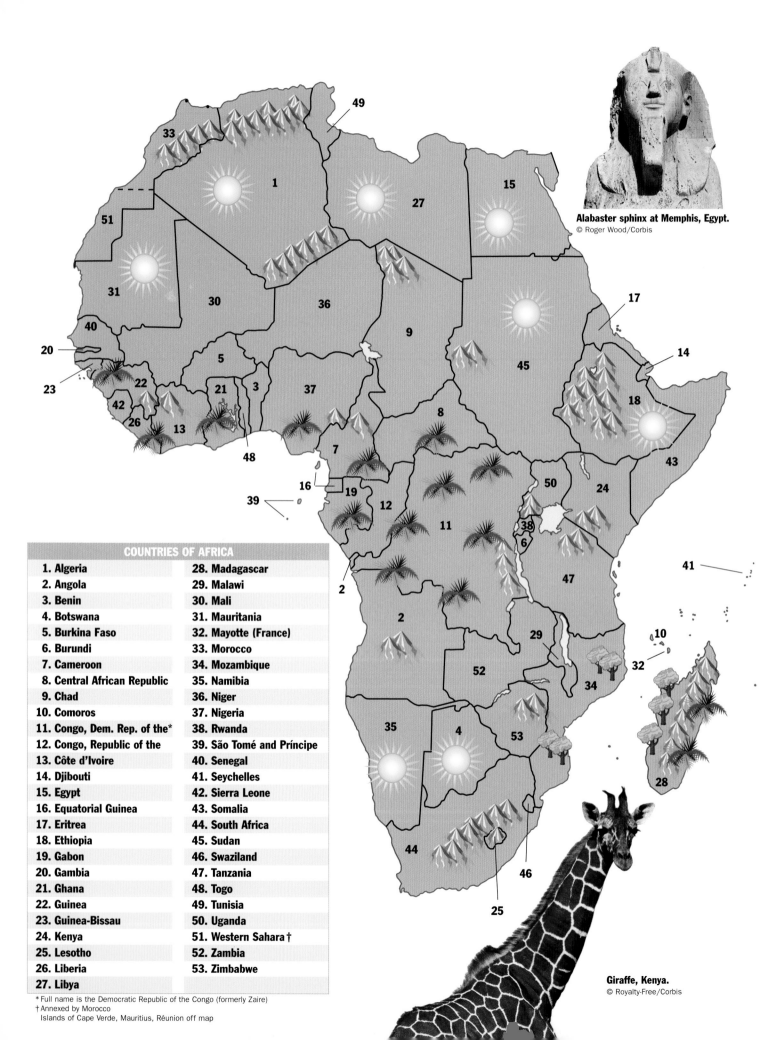

Alabaster sphinx at Memphis, Egypt.
© Roger Wood/Corbis

COUNTRIES OF AFRICA

1. Algeria
2. Angola
3. Benin
4. Botswana
5. Burkina Faso
6. Burundi
7. Cameroon
8. Central African Republic
9. Chad
10. Comoros
11. Congo, Dem. Rep. of the*
12. Congo, Republic of the
13. Côte d'Ivoire
14. Djibouti
15. Egypt
16. Equatorial Guinea
17. Eritrea
18. Ethiopia
19. Gabon
20. Gambia
21. Ghana
22. Guinea
23. Guinea-Bissau
24. Kenya
25. Lesotho
26. Liberia
27. Libya

28. Madagascar
29. Malawi
30. Mali
31. Mauritania
32. Mayotte (France)
33. Morocco
34. Mozambique
35. Namibia
36. Niger
37. Nigeria
38. Rwanda
39. São Tomé and Príncipe
40. Senegal
41. Seychelles
42. Sierra Leone
43. Somalia
44. South Africa
45. Sudan
46. Swaziland
47. Tanzania
48. Togo
49. Tunisia
50. Uganda
51. Western Sahara †
52. Zambia
53. Zimbabwe

* Full name is the Democratic Republic of the Congo (formerly Zaire)
† Annexed by Morocco
Islands of Cape Verde, Mauritius, Réunion off map

Giraffe, Kenya.
© Royalty-Free/Corbis

Land of Splendour

Africa's **splendour** is seen in its dramatic landscapes, its amazing animal life, and its **diverse** human culture. The African continent is the home of more than 800 million people living in more than 50 countries. Africa is the second largest continent on Earth, after Asia.

Africa's long coastline is shaped by the Atlantic and Indian oceans and the Mediterranean and Red seas. In the north of the continent lies the Sahara. It is the world's largest desert and covers almost all of northern Africa. Located in south-western Africa are two other major deserts, the Kalahari and the Namib.

The African continent has two major rivers, the Nile and the Congo. The Nile is the longest river in the world. At the southern end of the Nile is Lake Victoria, Africa's largest lake. Not far to the south-east of Lake Victoria is Mount Kilimanjaro, the highest point in Africa. One of the world's major waterfalls, Victoria Falls, is also in Africa.

Africa is known for its wildlife. There are elephants, rhinoceroses, hippopotamuses, lions, and leopards. Other animals include antelope, gazelles, giraffes, baboons, gorillas, hyenas, and chimpanzees. Most of these animals live in Africa's open grasslands or in tropical rainforests.

The people of Africa belong to hundreds of **ethnic** groups. Each group has its own language, traditions, religion, arts, and history. During its political history, Africa has been the site of Egyptian dynasties, African kingdoms, European colonies, and independent countries.

LEARN MORE! READ THESE ARTICLES…
ALGERIA · CONGO · SOUTH AFRICA

DID YOU KNOW?
Surprisingly, the coastline of Africa is shorter than the coastline of Europe, the second-smallest continent. This is because Africa has few inlets, large bays, or gulfs - features that add to coastal length by causing 'detours' away from a straight coastline.

SEARCH LIGHT

Find and correct the mistake in the following sentence: Africa is one of the smallest continents.

Answer: Africa is one of the largest continents.

How did the Congo get its name?

Women gather firewood in the Democratic Republic of the Congo, which is also called Congo (Kinshasa). More than two-thirds of the people live in small towns and villages.
© Gallo Images/Corbis

DID YOU KNOW?
The Congo River is one of the great rivers of the world. Only the Amazon River (in South America) drains a larger area than the Congo River does.

8

Two Countries, One Name

Congo (Brazzaville).

Congo (Kinshasa).

As long as 25,000 years ago, people began to live in the forests of the Congo River **basin** in west-central Africa. They gathered food from the forests and dug up roots to eat.

Today the Congo basin contains two countries separated by the Congo River. Both of the countries are called Congo. To tell them apart, they are sometimes referred to by the names of their capital cities. One of the countries is called Congo (Brazzaville), and the other is Congo (Kinshasa). Congo (Brazzaville) is officially known as the Republic of the Congo. Congo (Kinshasa) is officially called the Democratic Republic of the Congo.

The Congo region got its name from the Kongo, or Bakongo, one of the main groups of people who live there. These people have been in the area for centuries, from the time when the Congo was ruled by various kingdoms.

The Portuguese arrived in the kingdom called Kongo in 1483. At first the newcomers were friendly to the people of the kingdom. By the 1530s, however, the Portuguese were sending the Kongolese away as slaves.

By the late 1800s other European countries had become interested in the Congo region. They valued the Congo River as a route for trade between the west coast of Africa and the interior part of the continent. The French and the Belgians took over different parts of the Congo. The local people didn't win their independence until 1960. Though free, each of the two Congos faced many problems. Both countries experienced periods of fierce internal fighting and struggles for power.

LEARN MORE! READ THESE ARTICLES...
GHANA • GUINEA • KAMPALA, UGANDA

Brazzaville
⭐Kinshasa

These miners work at the Ashanti gold mine in Obuasi,
Ghana. Ghana has long been one of the world's leading
producers of gold. Mining provides work for many
of Ghana's people.

© Penny Tweedie/Corbis

SEARCH LIGHT

Why do you
think people
from so many other
countries wanted
to take over Ghana?
(Hint: Think of
Ghana's former name.)

Gold Coast of Africa

 The country of Ghana has so much gold that it was once called the Gold Coast of Africa. It still has the largest gold **reserves** in the world. Ghana is in western Africa. Accra is its capital and largest city.

Ghana has coastal plains in the south, **savannah** in the north, and hills and rainforests in between. The oddly shaped baobab tree grows in the savannah and coastal plains. There you will also find giant anthills, some of which are over 4 metres high. In the rainforests are tall trees such as the mahogany. And there are many kinds of animals - lions, leopards, elephants, buffalo, monkeys, and snakes, to name a few.

Many of Ghana's people work in fishing, logging, or gold mining. Farming is very important as well. Much of the farmland is used for growing cacao. These trees produce cocoa beans, which are used to make chocolate. Cacao, timber, and gold are sold to other countries.

Long ago the Almoravids from northern Africa conquered Ghana and forced its people to become slaves. Since then, many other groups have gone to Ghana. The Portuguese arrived in the 1400s. They traded in gold, ivory, and slaves. Later came the British, the French, the Dutch, the Swedes, and the Danes. In 1901 the British made the Gold Coast a **colony**. In 1957 the colony won its independence and became the new country of Ghana. Today Ghana is one of Africa's leading **democracies**.

Accra

LEARN MORE! READ THESE ARTICLES...
ACCRA, GHANA • LIBERIA • NIGERIA

DID YOU KNOW?

Ghana's weavers are famous for their colourful kente cloth, which is made in narrow strips in beautiful patterns. The patterns have such names as 'thousand shields', 'the lion catcher', and 'gold dust'. The strips are sewn together to make clothing.

 Answer: Ghana was called the Gold Coast for its vast reserves of gold. Throughout its history, many different people have wanted to control Ghana so that they could take its gold.

From Trading Post to Modern City

Accra is the capital of the West African country of Ghana. It lies on the coast of the Gulf of Guinea, which is part of the Atlantic Ocean. The city is built partly on a low cliff. The rest of it spreads northward across the Accra plains.

Accra reflects the cultures of the many people who have settled in the area where it now stands. The Ga people had villages there when the Portuguese arrived in 1482. The British, the Danes, and the Dutch came later. The Europeans built **fortified** trading posts along the coast. They traded in gold, ivory, and slaves. Because of the area's gold, it became known as the Gold Coast. In 1877 Accra became the capital of the British Gold Coast colony.

Children in Ghana enjoying a game called *mancala*, played with stones and cups.
© Margaret Courtney-Clarke/Corbis

The Gold Coast gained its independence from British rule in 1957 and took the name Ghana. Accra became the capital of the new country. Today it is a modern city of more than 1.5 million people.

Accra is Ghana's business and educational centre. The national museum and national **archives** and the Accra Central Library are located in the city. The University of Ghana is in nearby Legon. Black Star Square is the site of the Independence Arch. This large square is used for parades. For those who like sport, Accra has a football stadium and a racecourse. Not far from Accra are the Aburi **Botanical** Gardens, which were created by the British more than 100 years ago. And the city's large open markets receive most of the food supply each day.

LEARN MORE! READ THESE ARTICLES…
ANGOLA • GHANA • NIGERIA

DID YOU KNOW?
Accra's name comes from *nkran*, a word in the language of the Akan people of Ghana. *Nkran* are black ants that are found all over the city and the surrounding area.

SEARCH LIGHT

Which of
the following can
be said of Accra?
a) The British once
   ruled there.
b) It is located on the
   Pacific Ocean.
c) Part of the city is
   built on a cliff.

Accra lies along the Gold Coast, an area in southern Ghana that has rich deposits of gold. The Portuguese built this strong fort, now called Elmina Castle, in the Gold Coast in 1482. They wanted to keep all of the area's gold trade for themselves.

© Liba Taylor/Panos Pictures

Answer: The British once ruled there.
Part of the city is built on a cliff.

13

Forests and Minerals

Guinea is a country in western Africa on the Atlantic Ocean. Its capital city, Conakry, is a major port. Ships stop there to load up on Guinea's minerals and other products and transport them to markets around the world.

The land is divided into four main areas. A flat plain lies along the coast. Northern Guinea has open grasslands called savannahs. The grass there grows as high as three metres during the rainy season. To the east the Fouta Djallon **highlands** rise sharply from the plain. In the south-east is a hilly area with large forests. There are valuable teak, mahogany, and ebony trees in this area. But much of the forest is becoming open grassland because people have cut down many of the trees so that they can use the land for farming.

Most people in Guinea work as farmers, growing their own food. They grow rice, cassava, sweet potatoes, bananas, coffee, pineapples, peanuts, yams, and maize. Some crops are grown to sell to other countries. Guinea also has large amounts of such minerals as bauxite, iron ore, gold, and diamonds. These are mined and sold to other countries.

The people of Guinea belong to several different groups. In the Fouta Djallon region many people are Fulani. In northern Guinea are the Malinke. Other major groups in the country are the Susu, the Kissi, and the Kpelle. Until 1958 Guinea was a **colony** of France. Because of this the official language in Guinea is French. But many African languages are spoken there as well.

LEARN MORE! READ THESE ARTICLES…
CONGO • GHANA • NIGERIA

Conakry

SEARCH LIGHT

True or false? Most of the people in Guinea work as miners.

The savannahs of northern Guinea have some trees scattered among the grasses.
© David Reed/Panos Pictures

14

DID YOU KNOW?
All three of western Africa's major rivers begin in Guinea. The country's Fouta Djallon region is the source of the Niger, the Gambia, and the Senegal rivers.

Answer: FALSE. Most of the country's people are farmers.

Women try to catch fish in a small pond north of Monrovia, Liberia. Fish are a major source of protein for many Liberians.

© Jan Dago/Magnum Photos

Africa's Oldest Republic

In the 1820s some Americans who opposed slavery bought land in West Africa. They used it to create a new country for freed slaves, whose ancestors had been taken from Africa. This country was called Liberia. Its government was set up as a **republic** modelled on the United States government. Liberia is now the oldest republic in Africa. Despite the origins of the country, most of its citizens are not the descendants of former slaves.

Today you can find out about Liberia's past by visiting the Malima Gorblah Village and Besao Village. These villages preserve the country's old culture. They are like living museums of Liberia's past.

Liberia's climate is warm and humid all year and rainy from May to October. The country's forests and rolling hills are home to such wild animals as monkeys, chimpanzees, antelopes, elephants, crocodiles, and poisonous snakes. There are two rare animals found in Liberia. One is the pygmy hippopotamus, which looks like a baby hippo even when it is fully grown. The other is the manatee, a big seal-shaped **mammal** that lives in the water.

The rubber trees, coffee, and cocoa that grow in Liberia provide products that can be sold to other countries. Liberian farmers also grow rice, sugarcane, bananas, and yams. Liberia is rich in mineral resources. It is one of the world's leading producers of iron ore.

Liberia suffered through a **civil war** in the early 1990s. It made life dangerous and difficult for many people. The war officially ended in 1996, but some fighting has continued.

LEARN MORE! READ THESE ARTICLES...
GHANA · NIGERIA · SENEGAL

Monrovia

SEARCH LIGHT

Fill in the gap: Liberia is the oldest _____ in Africa.

Land of 500 Languages

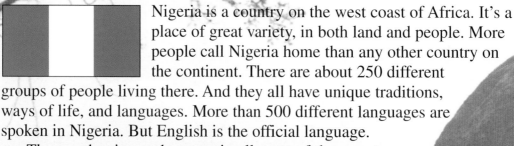

Nigeria is a country on the west coast of Africa. It's a place of great variety, in both land and people. More people call Nigeria home than any other country on the continent. There are about 250 different groups of people living there. And they all have unique traditions, ways of life, and languages. More than 500 different languages are spoken in Nigeria. But English is the official language.

The weather is not the same in all parts of the country. Some areas get a lot of rain. Other areas are very dry. Because there are different kinds of weather in different parts of the country, there are many kinds of animals and plants. There are thick **rainforests** as well as **mangrove** and freshwater swamps. There is also open grassland called the 'savannah'. There are small trees all over the **vast** savannah.

DID YOU KNOW?
It is said that more twins are born in Nigeria than anywhere else in the world. Twins are so common that they usually get the same set of names. For example, the Yoruba people usually name their twins Taiwo and Kehinde.

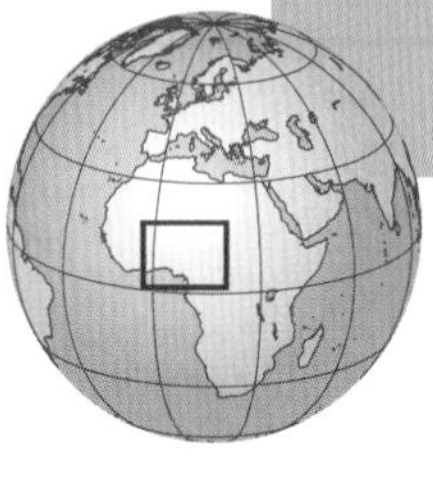

Wase Rock rises sharply above the surrounding countryside near Wase, Nigeria. This part of the country consists of savannah, or open grassland, with scattered short trees.
© Bruce Paton/Panos Pictures

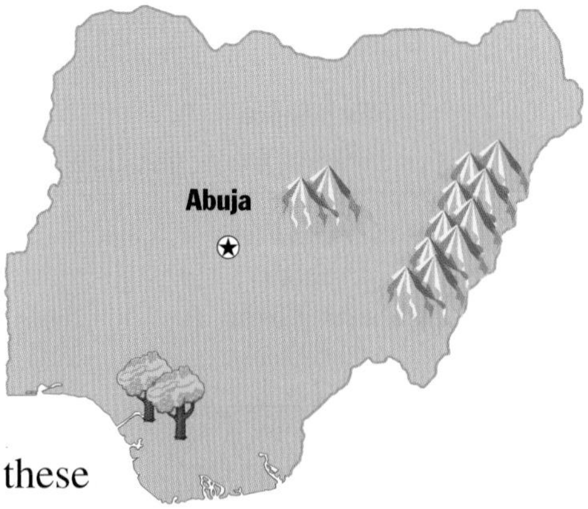

Abuja

Once, camels, antelope, hyenas, lions, baboons, and giraffes lived in the savannah. Red river hogs, forest elephants, and chimpanzees lived in the rainforest. Animals found in both forest and savannah included leopards, monkeys, gorillas, and wild pigs. Today these animals generally are found only in special parks.

Nigeria has many cities. The capital of Nigeria used to be Lagos. But in 1991 the capital changed to Abuja. Lagos is a very large coastal city with many businesses. But Abuja is in the middle of the country, which makes it easier for people to travel there. Lagos was overcrowded, too, and Abuja had more open land for building.

LEARN MORE! READ THESE ARTICLES...
CONGO • GHANA • SENEGAL

SEARCH LIGHT

True or false? Nigeria is a very rainy country.

Answer: FALSE. Parts of the country do get a lot of rain, but parts of it are very dry.

SEARCH LIGHT

The religion
followed by
most of the people
of Senegal is
a) Islam.
b) Christianity.
c) Buddhism.

A Soninke mother and child stand in the doorway of a traditional-
style mud house on a bank of the Senegal River. Like most of the
other peoples in Senegal, the Soninke are Muslim.

© Margaret Courtney-Clarke/Corbis

Land of Teranga

Long ago there was a house packed with men and women. They were inspected and priced like animals. The weaker ones died, and the stronger ones were shipped to the Americas to work as slaves. This slave house was on Gorée Island, which lies off the coast of Senegal, in westernmost Africa. Exactly what went on there is not known for sure. But Senegal was at one time involved in selling Africans as slaves.

Dakar

But that was long ago. Today Senegal's culture is known for its *teranga,* a spirit of warm welcome toward outsiders. *Teranga* means 'hospitality', or 'welcoming heart', in the language of the Wolof. Many different groups of people make up the Senegalese nation. The Wolof are one of the largest of Senegal's seven main **ethnic** groups.

Despite their different backgrounds, the people of Senegal tend to live in similar ways. Most of the people practice the religion of Islam. And most live in small villages in the countryside. Each village has a water source, a mosque (Islamic house of worship), and a public gathering place. France ruled Senegal until 1960. The different groups of Senegal speak several different African languages, but French is still widely used as a common language. This helps people from different groups talk to each other.

Senegal is one of the world's main producers of peanuts. The country has wide rivers and good soil. The light-coloured sandy soil in the north-western part of the country is especially good for growing peanuts. Dakar, the country's capital, is a major centre for the peanut trade.

DID YOU KNOW?
Léopold Senghor, the first president of independent Senegal, was also an important writer. He was a leading poet of a movement that celebrated African culture.

LEARN MORE! READ THESE ARTICLES...
GHANA • LIBERIA • NIGERIA

Answer: a) Islam.

SEARCH LIGHT

Find and correct the mistake in the following sentence. Ethiopia is a young country located in the Horn of Africa region of eastern Africa.

A village lies in a typically rugged part of Ethiopia's landscape.
© Jacques Langevin–Corbis/Sygma

Ancient Country in Africa's Horn

Not very long ago, a lot of people in Ethiopia, a country in eastern Africa, went hungry. In 1992-93 the Ethiopian government had to ask countries to donate food for its people. Some 10 million people faced starvation. Although many countries helped, hundreds of thousands of Ethiopians still suffered. Many later died because they had no food.

Most Ethiopians are farmers. But sometimes the government makes bad decisions on how to use the country's farmland. That's one reason why there's not always enough food to meet the needs of the people. Another reason is lack of rain. Ethiopia has two rainy seasons. But once in a while it suffers from droughts, times when it does not rain enough. Often Ethiopia must buy food from other countries. But Ethiopia sells things such as sugarcane, beeswax, leather goods, and coffee. Ethiopia is the place where coffee first came from.

Ethiopia is one of the oldest countries in Africa. It lies within a region that's called the Horn of Africa because on a map it looks like an animal's horn. The capital is Addis Ababa. Most of the people in Ethiopia are Christian. Some follow Islam. Others follow traditional animism, the belief that there is life in the forces of nature or even in **inanimate** objects.

One of the exciting things in Ethiopia is the rich variety of wildlife. But many of the animals have become rare, including lions, leopards, elephants, giraffes, rhinoceroses, and wild buffalo. In order to protect the remaining animals, the government has set aside 20 special parks and **sanctuaries**.

Addis Ababa

LEARN MORE! READ THESE ARTICLES…
ADDIS ABABA, ETHIOPIA • KENYA
MOGADISHU, SOMALIA

Answer: Ethiopia is an ancient country located in the Horn of Africa region of eastern Africa.

SEARCH LIGHT

How did Addis Ababa get so many eucalyptus trees?

The City Called 'New Flower'

If you visit Ethiopia by plane, you will probably land in Addis Ababa. The city is the capital of Ethiopia and its largest city. Addis Ababa sits high in the mountains at an **elevation** of about 2,450 metres above sea level. It is the highest city in Africa.

At one time in Ethiopia's history, a town called Entoto was the capital. This town had a cold **climate** but lacked enough firewood to provide heat

Wedding party, Addis Ababa.
© Michael S. Lewis/Corbis

for the people. The wife of Emperor Menilek II wanted him to build a house at a nearby hot springs. The emperor did so, and a new city was founded around it in 1887. The emperor's wife named the new city Addis Ababa, which means 'New Flower'.

As the population of Addis Ababa grew, that city experienced a shortage of firewood too. To help solve this problem, a large number of eucalyptus trees were imported from Australia. The eucalyptus trees eventually grew in number and now provide a forest for the city's needs.

Today Addis Ababa is the **headquarters** of several international organizations. One of them is the United Nations Economic Commission for Africa. Another one is the African Union. This league includes many African nations that work together to improve their economies and governments.

As a national capital, Addis Ababa has many of Ethiopia's government buildings. The city is also an important educational and commercial centre too. Addis Ababa University was started in 1950. And goods such as textiles, plastics, and wood products are **manufactured** in the city. Addis Ababa is also the site of one of Africa's largest open-air markets.

LEARN MORE! READ THESE ARTICLES…
ETHIOPIA • MOGADISHU, SOMALIA • NAIROBI, KENYA

Merchants sell traditional textiles at an outdoor market in Addis Ababa.
© Carl & Ann Purcell/Corbis

Answer: The city had many of the trees brought over from Australia to provide a source of firewood. Over time, the trees grew in number.

25

Cradle of Humanity

Some of the very earliest humans are believed to have lived in Kenya. That is why some people call the country the 'cradle of humanity'.

Kenya is a country in East Africa. Its capital is Nairobi. The country has a beautiful natural landscape with great variety. There are sandy beaches, huge mountains, rolling grassland, and deserts. A long deep valley cuts through western Kenya. It is part of the Great Rift Valley, a very long series of cracks in the Earth's surface. It runs from south-western Asia through East Africa. Part of Kenya's south-eastern border lies along the Indian Ocean. Lake Victoria makes up part of Kenya's western borders. It's the largest lake in Africa.

The Kenyans are mostly farmers. In the Mount Elgon region, coffee and tea are grown and then sold to other countries. Mount Elgon is a volcano that no longer erupts. The soil in this volcanic region is especially good for growing crops. In the evergreen forests in the west are valuable trees such as cedar and podo. In the south of the country, most of the forests have been cut down.

Kenya's wildlife safaris are world famous. Many tourists visit the country to see the wide range of wild animals, including lions, leopards, elephants, giraffes, gazelles, baboons, and many others. In the rivers there are hippopotamuses, crocodiles, and many fish and spiny lobsters. Many of the animals that live in Kenya are very rare. The country has set up more than 50 national parks and preserves to protect its wildlife.

LEARN MORE! READ THESE ARTICLES...
KAMPALA, UGANDA • MOGADISHU, SOMALIA • NAIROBI, KENYA

Nairobi

SEARCH LIGHT

Find and correct the error in the following sentence: Kenyan farmers are mainly known for their rice and cabbage crops.

A group of Masai men perform a traditional dance in Kenya. All young Masai men are brought up to learn the group's customs. They are also encouraged to develop strength, courage, and endurance - traits for which the Masai warriors are noted throughout the world.

© Wendy Stone/Corbis

DID YOU KNOW?

Every year more than a million wildebeests, a kind of African antelope, pass through Kenya.

Answer: Kenyan farmers are mainly known for their coffee and tea crops.

27

DID YOU KNOW?
Nairobi is the largest city between Johannesburg, South Africa, in the far south of the continent, and Cairo, Egypt, in northern Africa.

From Swamp to Capital City

Nairobi used to be a swampy place. But this swamp would one day become the capital city of Kenya in East Africa. The name Nairobi comes from a water hole that the Masai people of Kenya called Enkare Nairobi. Enkare Nairobi means 'cold water'.

In the late 1890s, the British established a settlement there while building a railway across southern Kenya. This railway still runs through

A mosque in Nairobi.
© Stephen Frink/Corbis

Nairobi. It connects Lake Victoria, on the border with Uganda, to Mombasa, Kenya's major **port** on the Indian Ocean. When the British took control of Kenya in 1905, Nairobi was made its capital city. Under British rule, Nairobi grew into a trading centre and a large city. It remained the capital when Kenya became free from the British in 1963.

Today Nairobi is an important centre for education. The University of Nairobi and its Kenyatta University College are among the major schools in the city. Visitors go to see the National Museum of Kenya, McMillan Memorial Library, and Kenya National Theatre. The **tourism** industry is important to the city's economy.

Just a few miles south of the city is Nairobi National Park. It's a large beautiful park set aside to protect the area's wild animals. It was the first such park established in Kenya. Tourists go to see the park's lions, black rhinoceroses, gazelles, giraffes, antelope, and zebras, as well as hundreds of kinds of birds. Near the main gate is a small zoo. Keepers there take care of baby elephants and black rhinoceroses.

LEARN MORE! READ THESE ARTICLES...
KAMPALA, UGANDA • KENYA • MOGADISHU, SOMALIA

Once just a swamp, Nairobi is now a large city with modern buildings.
© Adrian Arbib/Corbis

SEARCH LIGHT

Enkare Nairobi means
a) swampy place.
b) cold water.
c) hot city.

29

Answer: b) cold water.

About how many islands make up the Republic of Seychelles?

The rocky islands of the Seychelles are rugged and beautiful.
© Nik Wheeler/Corbis

An Island Paradise

The Republic of Seychelles is a country made up of about 115 islands in the Indian Ocean off the east coast of Africa. Victoria is its capital city and the only shipping port. It lies on Mahé, the country's largest island.

The Seychelles is made up of two main island groups. The Mahé group has 40 islands. These islands are rocky and hilly, with narrow strips of coastline. The other group consists of low islands built up from the rock-hard skeletons of countless coral animals. These coral islands have almost no water, and very few people live on them.

Mahé is home to the great majority of the country's people. Most of the people are Creole, with a mixture of Asian, African, and European heritage. The French and then the British used to rule the islands. The Seychelles was given its independence by Britain in 1976. Creole, English, and French are all national languages.

The islands have very little good farmland. Tree products such as coconuts and cinnamon bark are the main crops. Fishing is a very important industry. The people catch the fish, pack them into cans, and ship them around the world.

The islands are especially rich in beautiful **tropical** scenery. Coconut palm trees grow along the coast on most of the islands. Giant tortoises and green sea turtles live along the coasts. Sharks are found in the ocean. The seafaring frigate bird spends time on the islands. Tourism is the Seychelles' biggest industry, with visitors attracted by the country's beaches, wildlife, and greenery.

Victoria

LEARN MORE! READ THESE ARTICLES...
AFRICA • MADAGASCAR • MOGADISHU, SOMALIA

Seaside Somalian Capital

Mogadishu is the capital of Somalia, a country in eastern Africa. The city lies along the Indian Ocean. Mogadishu is a major port. It is also the largest city in the country.

A big part of the city is in ruins today. It is hard to think that at one time Mogadishu was a lively city with bright whitewashed walls. There were beautiful **mosques** topped by tall towers called 'minarets'. But years of internal fighting in Somalia have left the city a ghost of its former self.

Arab settlers from the Persian Gulf set up the city in about the 10th century. The city traded goods with the Arab states, the Portuguese, and the leaders of Muscat (Oman) in the Middle East. The city's trade grew to include Persia, India, and China. During that time the city grew wealthy and powerful. In the 16th century, the Portuguese saw the success of the city and wanted to own it. But they were never able to take it over. In the late 19th century, Italy was in charge of the city.

In 1960 Mogadishu became the capital of Somalia. By that time Somalia was independent. Building began in the new city. The style of the old buildings and mosques mixed well with the style of the new ones.

But a **civil war** broke out in Somalia starting in the 1980s. Many people died during the fighting, and there was damage everywhere.

LEARN MORE! READ THESE ARTICLES...
ADDIS ABABA, ETHIOPIA • KAMPALA, UGANDA • NAIROBI, KENYA

SEARCH LIGHT

Find and correct the mistake in the following sentence: Mogadishu, the capital of Somalia, is a young city.

Schoolchildren listen to a lesson in a classroom in Mogadishu.
© David Turnley/Corbis

DID YOU KNOW?

Mogadishu's prominent location has made it a port of call for many travellers. In the early 15th century, the famous Chinese admiral Zheng He stopped there on three of his voyages throughout the Indian Ocean.

SEARCH LIGHT

Fill in
the gap:
Kampala is
built on a
series of _____.

F2841

City on the Hill of Antelopes

Kampala is the capital and largest city of Uganda, a country of East Africa. It lies in the southern part of the country, north of Lake Victoria. Kampala spreads over a number of hills. The rulers of the powerful Buganda kingdom of the 1800s kept antelope on the slopes. In the local language, Kampala means 'the hill of antelopes'.

Buganda came under the control of the British in the 1890s. The British chose Kampala as the site of their headquarters. For a while they controlled all of what is now Uganda from a fort on Old Kampala Hill. When Uganda gained independence from Great Britain in 1962, Kampala became the capital.

Kampala

Kampala is Uganda's centre for business. It lies on **fertile** farmland and is the main market for the Lake Victoria region. Coffee, cotton, tea, tobacco, and sugar are sold there. And most of Uganda's large companies have their offices in the city.

Kampala serves as the religious centre for Uganda as well. Some well-known Christian churches in the city include the Namirembe Anglican **Cathedral** and Rubaga and St Peter's Roman Catholic cathedrals. Kampala's many **mosques** include the white Kibuli Mosque. It also has Hindu temples.

If you ever visit Kampala, make sure to go to the Uganda Museum. It has a collection of historical musical instruments that you can play. You'll also find a number of art galleries in the city. Northeast of Kampala, a place called Nyero is famous for a different kind of art. There you can see rock paintings that date back hundreds of years. No one knows for sure who made them.

LEARN MORE! READ THESE ARTICLES…
CONGO • KENYA • NAIROBI, KENYA

DID YOU KNOW?

The Kasubi Tombs, on a hill overlooking Kampala, are the burial place of the kings of the Buganda kingdom.

Ugandans shop for bananas at a market in Kampala. The city lies within Uganda's most important farming region.
© David and Peter Turnley/Corbis

Answer: Kampala is built on a series of hills.

Desert Land on the Sea

Algeria is a country on the north coast of Africa. It is the 2nd largest country in Africa and the 11th largest country in the world. The country's capital is Algiers.

Algiers

The northern part of Algeria is on the Mediterranean Sea. This area is known as the Tell. Two mountain ranges separate the coastal area in the north from the Sahara in the south. About four-fifths of Algeria's land lies within the Sahara, the largest desert in the world. Two huge sandy areas known as 'ergs' cover most of Algeria's desert. Not much grows on the desert's surface. But there are valuable minerals, **oil**, and gas underground.

Rainfall is very rare in the desert. At times, areas in the Sahara get no rain for years. There are also dry streambeds known as *wadi*s in the desert. If it rains, the *wadi*s quickly fill with water.

Most of Algeria's people live in the northern part of the country, where the climate is mild. That area receives enough water from rivers and rainfall to water the crops and provide people with water for drinking and industry. The people in Algeria are mostly Arabs, but many are Berbers. The ancestors of the Berbers lived in the area before the Arabs arrived.

Algeria was a French colony for more than 100 years. Hundreds of thousands of French people settled there. After a war against the French, the Algerians gained their independence in 1962. Most of the French then left the country.

LEARN MORE! READ THESE ARTICLES...
LIBYA • RABAT, MOROCCO • SENEGAL

SEARCH LIGHT

A *wadi*
is a
a) northern part
of the country.
b) dry streambed.
c) wide field of sand.

DID YOU KNOW?

The name Sahara comes from the Arabic word *sahra'*, which means 'desert'.

This trans-Saharan highway winds through the desert in Algeria. Historically, travelling through the Sahara was very slow and dangerous. But year by year modern roadways have been extended farther along the ancient trade routes into the desert.

© Robert Holmes/Corbis

Answer: b) dry streambed.

DID YOU KNOW?
More than 2 million blocks of stone had to be cut, transported, and assembled to create the Great Pyramid.

The Pharaohs and the Pyramids

Nearly 5,000 years ago there was a kingdom by the Nile River in a place called Egypt. The king was known as the pharaoh. People thought of him as a god.

The people of Egypt developed a great **civilization**. They built ships and sailed to other countries. They made great buildings. They carved and painted lovely pictures. And they developed a system of writing.

Three Egyptian kings - Khufu, his son Khafre, and his grandson Menkure - each ordered the people to build him a pyramid. The pyramids were to be the kings' **tombs**. A pyramid is a large structure with a square base and four sides shaped like triangles. The sides slope upward and meet in a point at the top.

After a king died, his body was carefully prepared and wrapped in many layers of cloth. (A body prepared in this way is called a 'mummy'.) Then it was placed in a splendid coffin that was placed in a room in the middle of the pyramid. The Egyptians believed in an afterlife. So they put all the pharaoh's treasures in the room too, for him to use in the afterlife. After that, the doors were sealed with stones.

The pyramids of the pharaohs can still be seen today. They stand by the Nile River near a town called Giza. The first pyramid to be built is perhaps the largest structure ever made by people. It is called the Great Pyramid. The other two pyramids stand beside it. It took thousands of workers many years to build the pyramids. But since the Egyptians had no heavy machinery, no one knows exactly how they were built.

LEARN MORE! READ THESE ARTICLES...
AFRICA • THE SUDAN • SUEZ CANAL, EGYPT

SEARCH LIGHT

Fill in the gap: Three kings of Egypt ordered that giant _____ be built to use as their tombs.

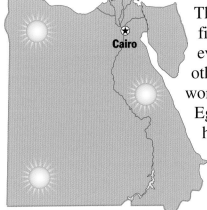

Cairo

In ancient times the pyramids built near Giza, Egypt, were counted among the Seven Wonders of the World.
© Larry Lee Photography/Corbis

Answer: Three kings of Egypt ordered that giant pyramids be built to use as their tombs.

39

Joining Two Seas for a Shortcut

The Suez Canal is one of the most important waterways that people have ever made. The **canal** is located in Egypt. It joins the Mediterranean Sea and the Red Sea and separates the continents of Africa and Asia. It offers the shortest route for ships sailing between Europe and the lands on the Indian and western Pacific oceans, such as Australia and large parts of Asia. Before the canal was built, ships travelling between these parts of the world had to sail all the way around Africa.

Beginning about 3,900 years ago, people dug several canals roughly in the area of the Suez Canal. But none of them joined the Mediterranean and Red seas directly. The Suez Canal was created by joining a series of lakes across the **Isthmus** of Suez to form one long water passage between the two seas.

Watching a ship pass through the Suez Canal.
© David & Peter Turnley/Corbis

The Suez Canal has eight major bends. In some places it has been widened to form double channels called 'bypasses'. These allow ships travelling in opposite directions to pass each other. In the canal ships travel in groups and follow rules to prevent accidents. Each ship moves at a set speed, leaving a fixed gap between it and the next ship in the group. This keeps the ships from knocking against each other. A tugboat follows each large ship. The entire trip takes between 12 and 18 hours.

On average, 50 ships cross through the Suez Canal each day. Nearly 20,000 trips are made in a year. Most of the vessels using the canal are small tankers and cargo ships, though some passenger liners and warships also use the waterway.

LEARN MORE! READ THESE ARTICLES...
AFRICA • ALGERIA • EGYPT

SEARCH LIGHT

Fill in the gaps: The Suez Canal joins the _____ Sea with the _____ Sea.

Cargo ships like this one make up a large part of the traffic in the Suez Canal.
Hubertus Kauns/Superstock

DID YOU KNOW?

By taking the Suez Canal shortcut, a ship travelling from London, England, to Bombay, India, cuts more than 8,000 kilometres off its trip.

Oil Country of Africa

Libya was once a poor country. Then in 1959 petroleum, or crude **oil**, was discovered in the desert. This made Libya one of the richest countries in North Africa. Some of the largest oil deposits in the world are in Libya. The capital city of Libya is Tripoli. It is located on the coast of the Mediterranean Sea and is one of Libya's major ports.

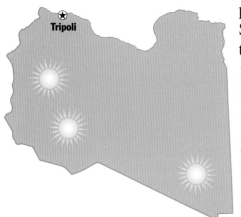

Libya has three main regions: the Sahara, Tripolitania, and Cyrenaica. The largest is the desert land of the Sahara, which is one of the driest places on Earth. There are very few plants in the Sahara. However, date palms grow in the oases, such as that found around the town of Sabha. An oasis is a **fertile** place in the desert where water can be found. Most Libyans live in Tripolitania, in the north-west. Many of the people keep sheep and goats. They also grow barley, wheat, tobacco, dates, figs, grapes, and olives. In Cyrenaica, in the north-east, the Akhdar Mountains and some oases are the main features.

Many people in Libya identify themselves with traditional tribes, or *qabilah*s. The Berbers, the original people of Libya, were mostly coastal farmers. Today, however, most Libyans have a mixed Berber and Arabic **heritage**.

Libya became an independent country in 1951. It was ruled by a king until 1969. In that year a group of army officers led by Muammar al-Qaddafi took control of the country. Many people outside Libya have criticized Qaddafi for supporting terrorists and using his army to attack other countries.

LEARN MORE! READ THESE ARTICLES...
EGYPT • RABAT, MOROCCO • THE SUDAN

SEARCH LIGHT

Libya has been a much wealthier country since
a) oil was discovered.
b) gold was discovered.
c) water was discovered.

DID YOU KNOW?

The highest temperature ever recorded on Earth was measured at Al-Aziziyah, Libya. One day in September 1922, the temperature soared to 58°C.

A lake lined with palm trees forms an oasis in the Libyan desert.
Doug McKinlay/Lonely Planet Images

Answer: a) oil was discovered.

Built for Victory

Rabat is the capital city of Morocco, a country in North Africa. It is located on the coast of the Atlantic Ocean. Modern Rabat has a rich mixture of cultures reflecting African, Arab, Islamic, and French influences.

Rabat has ancient roots. The city started out almost 900 years ago as a camp for Muslims who wanted to sail across the sea to fight in Spain. Later, the camp was named Ribat al-Fath, which means 'camp of victory'. A wall was built to protect the camp. Within the wall the city of Rabat began to grow.

Large parts of the old wall are still standing. Within them are the old town and the Jewish quarter. The Oudia Gate and the Tower of Hassan also stand as impressive monuments of the past.

France and Spain each controlled sections of Morocco for part of the 20th century. The country gained its independence in 1956. Rabat now houses government offices, universities, and art schools. The king of Morocco lives in Rabat for part of the year.

It's a short ride by road or rail to Casablanca, which is Morocco's largest city and its chief port. Like Rabat, it was once a base for pirates who attacked European ships. The Portuguese put a stop to the piracy in 1468. They later built a new town in the area called Casa Branca. The French called it Maison Blanche, and the Spanish called it Casablanca. All these names mean the same thing: 'white house'.

LEARN MORE! READ THESE ARTICLES...
ALGERIA • EGYPT • LIBYA

SEARCH LIGHT

What ruler lives in the city of Rabat today?

DID YOU KNOW?

The name Rabat comes from the Arabic word *ribat*. That word is often translated as 'camp' but can also mean 'monastery'. In North Africa it refers to a place were Muslim soldiers would gather either to study or to prepare for holy war.

A wall built hundreds of years ago still surrounds part of the city of Rabat.
© Nik Wheeler/Corbis

Sudanese men rest on a wall near their camels, which are considered a symbol of wealth. Many people in The Sudan raise camels for their milk and meat as well as for transportation.
© Jonathan Blair/Corbis

46

Giant of Africa

The largest country in Africa is The Sudan. It is the tenth largest country in the world. The Sudan is located in north-eastern Africa. Khartoum is the capital city. It sits at the point where the Blue Nile and White Nile rivers join together to form the mighty Nile River. The Sudan is one of the hottest places in the world. In Khartoum temperatures higher than 38°C may be recorded during any month of the year.

There are 19 major **ethnic** groups in The Sudan. More than 100 languages and **dialects** are spoken in the country. Many of the people either farm or rear camels and cattle. Roughly 10 per cent of the people live as **nomads**. Amongst all groups poetry and song are respected art forms. Both often reflect the country's mixed Arab and African **heritage**.

In 1956 The Sudan gained its independence from the United Kingdom. But fighting broke out almost immediately. The people living in southern Sudan opposed the new government, which was controlled by northerners. The southerners are typically black Africans who practise traditional African religions or Christianity. The northerners are typically of mixed ethnic origins. They speak a version of Arabic and practise Islam. The fighting continued until 1972, when the southerners were given control of their local government. But war broke out again in 1983. In 2002 the two sides agreed to stop the war, but fighting continued in some parts of the country.

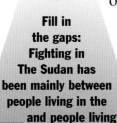

SEARCH LIGHT

Fill in the gaps: Fighting in The Sudan has been mainly between people living in the _____ and people living in the _____.

LEARN MORE! READ THESE ARTICLES…
EGYPT • ETHIOPIA • KENYA

An Angolan woman wears traditional dress.
Giacomo Pirozzi/Panos Pictures

SEARCH LIGHT

How were the Portuguese able to take control of Angola and stay in power there? (Hint: What would the Portuguese have brought with them to fight with?)

Land of Oil and Diamonds

Angola is a large country on the south-western coast of Africa. The Atlantic Ocean is its western boundary. Four countries shape its borders on land. Its capital is Luanda, a large city on the coast.

Most of Angola is a high **plateau** covered by savannahs, which are open grasslands with scattered trees. Roaming this land are leopards, lions, hyenas, elephants, and hippopotamuses. You may also see giraffes, zebras, and monkeys. With such rich wildlife, Angola has many national parks and nature **reserves**. However, some of the animals are in danger of disappearing because of hunting and other reasons. These animals include elephants, gorillas, chimpanzees, and black rhinoceroses.

The two largest groups of people in Angola are the Ovimbundu and the Mbundu. These two groups, and others, speak different languages that together are called Bantu languages. Almost all of the people also speak Portuguese, the country's official language.

Angola has many natural resources. Two of them - oil and diamonds - are major parts of the country's **economy**. Angola sells these products to other countries. But more people work in farming than in any other job. They grow **cassava**, maize, sugarcane, bananas, and coffee. In the south-west they rear cattle.

Portuguese explorers reached Angola in 1483. Over time, the Portuguese developed a **colony**. They ruled for almost 500 years. During much of this time, the Portuguese sent millions of Africans away from the colony to work as slaves. After years of fighting the Portuguese, Angola finally won its independence in 1975. But afterward the country struggled off and on with fighting inside its borders.

LEARN MORE! READ THESE ARTICLES...
AFRICA • BOTSWANA • CONGO

DID YOU KNOW?
Angola is rich in tropical woods such as mahogany, rosewood, and black ebony. These woods are used to make fine furniture.

★ Luanda

Answer: In the 15th century, when Portugal conquered Angola, the Bantu-speaking peoples didn't have guns or cannons. The Portuguese had both.

SEARCH LIGHT

Why did
Botswana
become one
of Africa's
wealthiest countries?

The Jewel of the Kalahari

Botswana was once one of the poorest countries in Africa. It used to be called Bechuanaland. After gaining independence from Great Britain in 1966, it was renamed Botswana. The new name came from that of the main group of people living there, the Tswana, or Batswana. In 1967 large **deposits** of diamonds were discovered in the region. Suddenly Botswana was one of Africa's richest countries.

Botswana is located in southern Africa. Its capital city is Gabarone. Most of the country's area is a dry region called the Kalahari. This is known as the sandveld, or 'thirstland'. The thirstland is different from a true desert because it has some grass and trees. In eastern Botswana there are rocky ranges of hills.

In the north-west is the Okavango River, which flows in from Namibia. It has been called 'the river that never finds the sea' because it ends in Botswana instead of flowing into the ocean. The place where it ends is called the Okavango **delta**. This huge swampy area has thick clumps of **papyrus** and much wildlife, including lions, hippopotamuses, and zebras. Many of the animals are protected in the Moremi Wildlife Reserve.

Botswana has forests in the north and east. Some of the trees produce fruits such as the marula or nuts such as the mongongo, which are important to the diet of the local people. Their diet also includes beans, meat, and **porridge** made with sorghum or maize. Some people eat dried caterpillars as a snack!

Gabarone

DID YOU KNOW?
The San people of the Kalahari speak an unusual language. It's called a 'click language' because it has many clicking sounds as parts of words. It is nearly impossible to speak that language if you don't learn it while you are growing up.

LEARN MORE! READ THESE ARTICLES...
AFRICA • HARARE, ZIMBABWE • SOUTH AFRICA

Many people in Botswana live in small towns and villages such as this one in the Okavango delta region of the country.
© Yann Arthus-Bertrand/Corbis

SEARCH LIGHT

★

Where did the first people to live in Madagascar come from?

Island Sanctuary

The Republic of Madagascar lies more than 400 kilometres off the south-eastern coast of Africa in the Indian Ocean. It occupies the fourth largest island in the world; only Greenland, New Guinea, and Borneo are larger. The capital of Madagascar is Antananarivo. It is located in the centre of the country.

Even though Madagascar is so close to Africa, its people are not mainly African. The first people to live on the island were Malagasy people from Indonesia, almost 5,000 kilometres to the east. They arrived in about AD 700. People from Africa, Europe, and other parts of Southeast Asia came later. The people of Madagascar are still called Malagasy, but today their culture is a unique mix of Asian and African influences.

Antananarivo

About half of the Malagasy follow Christianity. Most of the rest practise a traditional religion that has been passed down through the years. These people believe that the dead can reward or punish the living. They bury the dead in richly decorated tombs. They spend more time, money, and care on building tombs than they do on their houses.

For thousands of years Madagascar was covered with forests. But over time most of the trees have been cut down to make room for rice fields. The loss of the forests has been difficult for many of the animals of Madagascar - especially the lemurs. Lemurs look something like monkeys with long bushy tails. They are found in the wild only in Madagascar and on nearby islands. Madagascar also has many unique kinds of birds, chameleons, and butterflies. There are about 800 types of butterflies alone!

LEARN MORE! READ THESE ARTICLES...
AFRICA • SEYCHELLES • SOUTH AFRICA

DID YOU KNOW?
The coelacanth, a fish thought to have been extinct for 60 million years, was found in the waters near Madagascar in the 1900s. Such animals are sometimes called 'living fossils' because their appearance and other physical traits have not changed for millions of years.

Rice fields line a hillside in Madagascar.
© Chris Hellier/Corbis

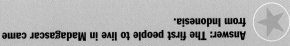
Answer: The first people to live in Madagascar came from Indonesia.

53

On Malawi's Fertile Plains

The capital of Malawi, a country in southern Africa, is Lilongwe. It is largely a planned city. It was not founded until 1947, when it was established as a trading centre. The city is in the central part of the country. In the late 1960s the leaders of Malawi decided to try to develop this central area of the country further. As part of their plan, they moved the capital from Zomba to Lilongwe in 1975.

In addition to being a government centre, Lilongwe provides a market for local farmers to sell their crops. Some of the country's best farmland surrounds Lilongwe. This region produces tobacco, the main crop that Malawi sells to other countries. In Lilongwe you can visit the tobacco auction floors, where large amounts of tobacco are sold.

The city has two main sections, the old city and Capital Hill. The old city has the central market, cafés, and restaurants. People go there regularly to shop. The newer part of the city, on Capital Hill, has government buildings, hotels, and **embassies**. Between the two sections of the city is a nature sanctuary, which provides protection for the native animals and plants. The sanctuary covers about 148 hectares and is home to many different kinds of birds.

Because of its central location, many people travel through Lilongwe on their way to other parts of the country. The city has an international airport. It also has rail connections to Salima in the east and the Zambian border on the west.

LEARN MORE! READ THESE ARTICLES...
BOTSWANA • HARARE, ZIMBABWE • WINDHOEK, NAMIBIA

DID YOU KNOW?

Although it is Malawi's capital, Lilongwe is only the second largest city in the country. Blantyre, in the south, is the largest city in Malawi and also the main centre of industry and commerce.

Lilongwe

Tobacco is sold at an auction in Lilongwe. The city is the centre of Malawi's tobacco processing and trading industries. Malawi is one of Africa's top tobacco producers.
David Else/Lonely Planet Images

Answer: Lilongwe is where tobacco, the country's main crop, is sold.

Namibia's Windy Corner

Windhoek is the capital city of Namibia, a country in southern Africa. The city lies at a height of more than 1,654 metres. It is surrounded by a ring of hills. These hills protect it from the most violent of the dry winds blowing in from the Kalahari Desert to the east and the Namib Desert to the west. The city's name comes from a German word that means 'windy corner'. Windhoek is free of fiercely blowing winds for less than four months of the year.

The Herero and Khoekhoe peoples were among the first settlers in the region. Before the Europeans arrived, the city was called Aigams. This name means 'hot water' and referred to the **hot springs** in the area.

Germany claimed the town for itself in 1890. South Africa took over the region, then known as South West Africa, 25 years later. When Namibia became independent in 1990, Windhoek was made the nation's capital.

Windhoek is also the country's chief economic centre. It sits in the middle of the grazing lands of the Karakul sheep. The skins of very young Karakul lambs are processed and transported by a number of furriers in Windhoek. This business employs many people in the city.

Windhoek has several interesting places and buildings to visit. The Alte Feste (Old Fort), built by the Germans, is one of the oldest buildings in the city. It is now a history museum. Christuskirche is an attractive church that was also built during German colonial times. And the city's St George's Cathedral is the smallest functional **cathedral** in southern Africa.

LEARN MORE! READ THESE ARTICLES…
AFRICA • BOTSWANA • SOUTH AFRICA

Windhoek

SEARCH LIGHT

Among the area's first residents were
a) Germans and South Africans.
b) Aigams and Namib.
c) Herero and Khoekhoe.

These buildings on a street in Windhoek display a mixture of styles, some modern and some from the time when Germany controlled the town.
© Royalty-Free/Corbis

DID YOU KNOW?
Mahatma Gandhi led his first political protest in South Africa. Before Gandhi began fighting for India's independence from Britain, he lived for a time in South Africa. He helped the Indians who lived there fight for their rights.

A People Apart

For several hundred years, most of South Africa's people had few freedoms. There are four main groups of South Africans today: black Africans, white Africans, people whose families came from India, and people of mixed origins. The whites make up a fairly small number of the country's people. But for a long time they held all the power. Nonwhites had many of their basic rights taken away.

In the 1650s the Dutch set up the first permanent European settlement in South Africa. The British and Dutch fought for control over the area during the 1800s. In 1910 the British established the Union of South Africa. Black Africans, the **majority** of the population, were not allowed to vote or hold political office.

In 1948 the government introduced a policy called apartheid. The word apartheid means 'apartness' in the Dutch language of Afrikaans. This policy gave most of the country's land to white people. Black Africans and other nonwhites were forced to live in separate areas and could enter areas where whites lived only if they had a pass. They had separate and worse schools and could hold only certain jobs. They could not vote or take part in government.

One of the leaders in the fight against apartheid was Nelson Mandela. Because of this, the government jailed him from 1962 to 1990. But black Africans continued to support Mandela. The country began to do away with apartheid in 1990. Mandela became South Africa's president in 1991, and he became a symbol of freedom throughout the world. The country's laws now support equal rights for everyone. But South Africa is still recovering from the effects of the many years of apartheid.

LEARN MORE! READ THESE ARTICLES...
AFRICA • ANGOLA • WINDHOEK, NAMIBIA

SEARCH LIGHT

Find and correct the mistake in the following sentence: Under apartheid, most of South Africa's land was reserved for nonwhites.

President Nelson Mandela celebrates with a choir after signing South Africa's new constitution in December 1996. The constitution promised equal rights for all of the country's people.
© Charles O'Rear/Corbis

Answer: Under apartheid, most of South Africa's land was reserved for whites.

DID YOU KNOW?

Girls in Zimbabwe used to start wearing jewellery at a young age and never take it off. As they grew older, they would simply add more beads and bangles to their jewellery. Some women would end up wearing more than 20 kilos of jewellery.

City in a Garden

Harare is the capital of the African country of Zimbabwe. It lies on a broad high ridge called the Highveld in the country's north-eastern garden region. Harare is green with trees and bright with flowers.

The city was founded in 1890. It was named Salisbury after Lord Salisbury, the British prime minister. As with much of southern Africa, Zimbabwe came under British rule in the late 1890s. The city developed only after 1899, when a railway line was established from the port of Beira in Mozambique to the east.

There were many industries that were started in Salisbury after World War II. People started moving into this city, and gradually the population grew. The city itself is modern and well planned, with high-rise buildings and tree-lined avenues.

In 1980 the new government of independent Zimbabwe renamed the city Harare. This honoured Chief Neharawe, who originally occupied this area with his people. The word Harare means 'one that does not sleep' in the Shona language.

Harare is still the centre of Zimbabwe's industry and **commerce**. It is the main place where crops from the surrounding farmlands are received and then distributed. There are also important gold mines nearby.

The University of Zimbabwe is located in Harare. The city is also home to the National Archives, which displays historical documents. At the National Gallery of Zimbabwe you can see an impressive collection of African painting and sculpture. And every year the city holds the Harare International Festival of the Arts. At this festival you can see all kinds of artistic performances, from traditional dancing and drumming to the plays of William Shakespeare.

LEARN MORE! READ THESE ARTICLES...
BOTSWANA • SOUTH AFRICA • WINDHOEK, NAMIBIA

SEARCH LIGHT

Harare is located on the
a) high seas.
b) Highveld.
c) highway.

Modern high-rise buildings loom over the city of Harare, Zimbabwe.
Richard I'Anson/Lonely Planet Images

Answer: b) Highveld.

G L O S S A R Y

archives place where public records or historical documents are kept

basin in geography, the area of land drained by a river and its branches

botanical (noun: botany) having to do with plant life

canal artificial waterway for boats or for draining or supplying water to land

cassava tropical plant that has a thick underground root-like part and can be made into a number of foods

cathedral large Christian church where a bishop is in charge

civil war war between opposing groups of citizens of the same country

civilization the way of life of a people at a particular time or place; also, a fairly advanced culture and technology

climate average weather in a particular area

colony (plural: colonies; adjective: colonial; verb: colonize) 1) in general, a settlement established in a distant territory and controlled by a more powerful and expanding nation; 2) in biology, a group of similar organisms that live together in a particular place

commerce (adjective: commercial) the buying and selling of goods, especially on a large scale and between different places

delta large triangular area made of material deposited at the mouth of a river, where it empties into the sea

democracy (adjective: democratic) government in which the highest power is held by the citizens; they either use their power directly (usually by voting) or choose others to act for them

deposit substance laid down by a natural process

dialect one of several varieties of a language used by the members of a particular group or class of people

diverse varied; different

economy the system in a country or group by which goods are made, services are offered, and both are sold and used

elevation the height of an object above sea level (that is, the surface of the ocean)

embassy the living quarters or office of an ambassador (a person who officially represents his or her own government in a foreign country)

ethnic having to do with a large group of people who share a racial, national, tribal, religious, language, or cultural background

fertile rich and productive; able to yield quality crops in large quantities

fortify to strengthen with weapons and by military defences

headquarters the governing and directing centre of an organization

heritage background or descent

highland high or mountainous land

hot spring a source of hot water coming from underground

inanimate not living

isthmus narrow strip of land connecting two larger land areas

majority most; usually, more than half of a group of individual people or things

mammal class of warm-blooded animals that feed their young with milk from special mammary glands, have an internal backbone, and are more or less covered with hair

mangrove tropical tree or shrub that has partly exposed roots and grows thickly in areas of salty water

manufacture to make from raw materials, by hand or by machine

mosque Muslim place of worship

nomad member of a people who have no permanent home but instead move from place to place, usually with the seasons and within a specific area

oil liquid taken from the ground and not yet cleaned or separated into such products as petrol and paraffin; also called petroleum

papyrus tall reed plant that grows in the Nile valley and that the ancient Egyptians used to make an early kind of paper

plateau wide land area with a fairly level surface raised sharply above the land next to it on at least one side

porridge soft food made by boiling grain meal or a vegetable in milk or water until it thickens

port protected harbour where ships dock to load or unload goods

rainforest dense tropical woodland with a high yearly rainfall and very tall trees

republic form of government in which citizens are allowed to elect officials and representatives responsible for governing by law

reserve area of land set apart for some special purpose; also (usually plural: reserves), money or valuable items kept in hand or set apart until needed

sanctuary safe place

savannah hot, dry grassland with scattered trees

splendour something very grand or beautiful

tomb special building or room in which a dead person is buried

tourism business of encouraging travel to a specific location and of managing services for visitors (including lodging, transport, food, and activities)

tropical having to do with the Earth's warmest and most humid (moist) climates

vast huge or spacious

I N D E X